Hold Your Breath

An Oncologist's Diary

Rana Bitar, MD. MFA

An earlier draft of this piece was submitted to and belong to the
Women Writing History: A Coronavirus Journaling Project, a
project of the National Women's History Museum.

Attention schools and businesses: for discounted copies on large
orders, please contact the publisher directly.

Unsolicited Press
Portland, Oregon
www.unsolicitedpress.com
orders@unsolicitedpress.com
619-354-8005

Front Cover Design: Kathryn Gerhardt
Editor: S.R. Stewart

ISBN: 978-1-956692-54-9

"Atop the broken universal clock:
The hour is crowed in lunatic thirteens.
Out painted stages fall apart by scenes
While all the actors halt in mortal shock:"

-Sylvia Plath-

Hold Your Breath

An Oncologist's Diary

March 16, 2020

Corona One

Have you ever thought of where you would want to be when and if the world was about to end? Have you thought about what you would have regretted doing or not doing? All the places you wanted to visit, and all the people you wanted to be with? All the words you wanted to write and all the books you wanted to read?

I was thinking about it this morning coming to work. *Where would I want to be?* The images that came to my mind were clear and immediate. I can see the place.

A few years ago, I suggested a location for a family vacation: Nova Scotia, Canada. It was April, and it was still cold there. The resort I picked sprawled generously by the ocean; lush fields of fresh green contrasted the blue of the water. It was supposed to be a golfing resort, but it wasn't the season yet. The place was almost empty. The majesty of the silence was crowned by the chanting of the waves, rising, then falling and breaking on the shore.

On the way to the resort, country roads ventured narrow and bumpy into farms on both sides. Tall turbines conversed with the wind and danced around and around and around in the arms of the clear blue sky. Living beings were scarcely spotted, except for horses and cows: they decorated the serenity of the scene sparsely with white and black and brown.

The setting was just the way I like it.

Although I am a city girl, my heart is planted in the soil of some distant farm, and my soul is scattered in the seawater among the bubbles of the fishes. So Nova Scotia was heaven to me; farms and water: my heart and soul came together: I felt at home.

My husband and two kids hated it. The emptiness and quietness during the day unnerved them. The ocean wind's whispers spooked them at night. There were no places for activities or dining outside the resort, so they found some entertainment by going to the spa and the pool and the game room. I never liked those kinds of things, so I bunkered at my temporary home. In that remote corner at the tip of North America, in that family suite with a fireplace and a balcony on the water, I had the time of my life. I spent my hours reading and writing by the ocean, fighting the wind in my hair and the chills in my bone, and absorbing that silence in my cells as if it was a life given to me unexpectedly.

Now you would think I should have felt guilty about it, but I didn't. Selfish me! The kids still talk about that trip and poke fun at me, and we laugh about it. And until this day, when I suggest places to go on vacation, they bring up the trip to Nova Scotia and take any of my suggestions skeptically.

If the world is going to end, I want to be there, giving my soul to the water and my hair to the wind and my heart to the fresh soil. And dreaming that I am a horse running over the clouds because there is no earth underneath me any longer.

March 18, 2020

Corona and Cancer

How much time do I have? The man asks.
With words muffled behind my double mask,
I mumble something. He accepts the answer,
the non-answer.
Sometimes, you ask just to hear the question
and not the response.
Is death disguised in the cancer cells inside him?
Or is it floating in the air around us?
I give him chemotherapy to chase away the first.
I wear a mask to trap out the second.
Equal fight?
Unknown.
The answer hides behind the mask of uncertainty.
What I had mumbled was:
How much time does life on Earth have?
I am glad he didn't hear it.
He is glad too.

Talking to people behind masks is tricky.
They can only see your eyes
and the frown in them can't hide behind a smile.
Truth. The truth is more naked behind a mask.

I feel each breath I take. How precious life is behind a mask!
Unmasked, you're never aware of breathing.
I hear my breath behind a mask.
How loud life is behind a mask!

Masks don't cover your vision. Only your gasp.
Google statistics.
Roll, roll, numbers roll. County's count. State's count.
Nation's count. World's count.
In the beginning, I could add and subtract
yesterday's cases from today's. How many more?
Now I can't. With six digits, you lose track.

No. You won't lose your job,
I answer my single-mother secretary.
Did she smile? Can I see her mouth behind her mask?
Did she see the truth in my eyes?

Thank God for masks.
No one questions the truth in the eyes
if it doesn't come out of the mouth.

How many masks do I have?
I have to make some from scratch this weekend.

MARCH 20, 2020

Self-Quarantine

Isolation's color bleeds into the hallways of my house
to the streets of my town, to the plazas and the bridges
and the parks and the museum's stairs and all the stop signs.

It paints the chairs and the tables
and the drive-through windows
and the countertops and the clothes racks
and the smiles of my children.

And I can't decide *what is the color of isolation?*
Blue like my mask? White like my coat?
Green like my scrubs? What is the smell of isolation? Sterility?
Sanitizers? Chloride?
Plastic breathing mask? Nasal oxygen tubes?
The Advil bottle on my nightstand?

Six feet apart. Rooms apart. *What is the shape of isolation?*
Is it the ache for a hug. For a kiss? Does ache have a shape?
Maybe it looks like a crumbled surgical glove
thrown in the "Hazardous Materials" bin.

MARCH 22, 2020

Quarantined

My mother used to say,
if you pluck one white hair off your head,
ten will grow in its place.
I wonder, does this apply to memories?
What do I do then, I asked. *Dye the white roots*, she said.
Is there a special chemical for coloring memories?

I invade the cabinet;
photo albums lay dormant there for years.
I tease the tranquility and shake the stillness.
Dust atop the thick brown covers yawns,
then protests with a blow into my nose.
I sneeze in my elbow as they say we should.
What would a limbless sneezer do in the time of Corona?
Can I blow that dust off, freely now
without body parts in the way?
I conquer the pages, flip after flip, looking
for a 20-year old photo to send to a friend.
Memories bleed behind the plastic pockets.
Quick. Quick. Bury them.

They say
there aren't enough funeral homes to bury corpses now.
Cremation it is.
Ashes will be the background
of my future photos.

My sister peaks from behind an old photograph.
No tears for you now, she announces.
Where are they? I ask.
She empties a sack she carries on her back.
Colored buttons tumble down on a silver tray.
She pushes it in my face.
Here are some of them; the rest I stitched onto the coat of the
wind.

Grief needs space to stretch so you can dress its limbs.

Where have you been hiding all this time?
Greif floats luxuriously on my spinal fluid;
it is taking a bubble bath:
a luxury not to be compared to a quick shower
in the tears of the eyes.

The foam tickles my nerves.

I have always been curious:
what happens after one dies.
The problem is one can't find that out more than once.

But now, in quarantine, I kind of understand. Solitude
in between four walls, roof, and ground. Between
wake and sleep; between alive and dead. Pretty fascinating.
Sounds come muffled behind the door:
someone is asking if I want something to drink.

The silence grants your thoughts a stage
to a play you have never seen before.
Thoughts come out to have a meal;
they sit around the table chat, eat, and drink: uninterrupted.
You hear the silverware clinking. Hush. Listen carefully,
lest you may miss the plot.
Can't do this if you weren't quarantined.
Almost dead, but alive. I savor it.

I can't do this on a normal day.

Tomorrow, I go back to work.
I got the mask I had ordered three months ago.
You could say I was in tune with China's news.
I was paranoid three months ago.
Now, I am brilliant.
*We always make characters of people retrospectively, depending on
the outcome.*

N-99 mask. Bulletproof.
*My friend, who asked for the old photo, doesn't like guns
metaphors.*

Do I wear it tomorrow?
It would be like wearing a Rolex to a fundraising event
to alleviate world's hunger.
I think I will keep it in my treasure box
and wear my five-day-old surgical mask.
I will save this one for another outbreak
when the mortality rate is more than 50%.

MARCH 31, 2020

Viral Dream

Daddy's face was our Central Park.
We ran on the banks of his mouth.
We sledded on the hill of his nose.
We made faces at ourselves in the ponds of his eyes.
We jumped ropes behind his ears.
We biked through his cheeks,
and played hide and seek under his mustache.

But when he shaved and nicked his skin,
and cotton balls found a ground to hold
onto his face to stop the blood,
playtime was over:
Weariness slithered through our veins,
and cold chills sifted through our marrows. Until

he took them off,
lumped them in his hand,
and pretended to gobble them down—
white fluffs tinged with red.
We laughed, cautiously then:
Mighty God musing with cotton candies.

I see my father's face
spread on Central Park's sprouting grass.
White tents like his cotton balls
sprawled over the nicks to stop the blood.
Green and navy logo printed on the sides, but no cotton
candies in hands.
NYC, beauty queen,
Where do we run?
What ropes do we jump?
What hills do we ride or sled?
Where do we hide?
and what do we seek?

NYC, beauty queen,
Skies foggy, streets mute.
Hearts crouched where the moon is supposed to shine.
But no. I say, no. You can't
break at the edge of a disaster like a wave.
Rise. Get up. Kick like the insolent you are.
Make me laugh at my father's cotton balls.
Take them off his face so that I can play again.
Kick. Rise. Rise. Stand up.
Get up and dance, Bohemian that you are—
golden anklets under the night stars.

April 1, 2020

April 1st

The Sun, bright and warm; it will be a nice spring day today.
Birds are singing; their chirps will lift the sky.
Runners on the roads.
Bikers on the tracks.
Lovers holding hands.

I will go home and get my garden soil ready to plant.
I will go to the market and get seeds and pots.
I will greet the cashier
and help the high school girl load my truck.
My kids will come back from school.
I will hug and kiss them.
Will have dinner
together.

They will invite their friends to stay.
They will party on the porch while I am digging the ground.
They will make lemonade.
They will spread a picnic blanket under the trees,
and share a drink and a snack,
and laugh.

Fill your lungs with the young sprouts scenting the air.
Earth is waking up to our dreams.
A bouquet of flowers is hiding behind the tree.
Don't peek. Wait for it. Wait for it.
Wait for it.

April 2, 2020

Gravity's Pull

It gets harder, day after day
to push yourself up, out of the ground.
But you do. You get up and about. Your work
can't be done from home.

The air outside my house is thickened with nerves.
Quietness heavy as gravity.
Asphalt wears a long black face of mourning,
consoled intermittently by
a car, or two, or
two silhouettes, walking
six feet apart.
The scene is—like in horror movies—
soaked in slowness:
Molecules drag and stretch each other,
extending a lingering fear that seems to never end.

I push the gate to my office building open
with my elbow.
It is getting harder to press forward with hands.
The doors of the exam rooms in my clinic stand tall
like scarecrows;
their knobs stare at me with malicious contempt.

Do I disinfect before? Or after I turn them? Or Both?

I listen to my patients' lungs:
Take a deep breath in   and out
I hold mine.

When we were kids, I competed with my brother:
on how long we each can hold our breaths.
I always won, until
his breath was held forever by a train crossing a car
He was sixteen.
The world stopped then, but didn't.
The train's whistle scratches my thoughts still
like chalk on a blackboard.
Holding my breath longer is the only thing
that is getting easier.

We are all in this together, true,
but cancer patients negotiate with two forms of death:
One peeks out from their insides,
and one hovers over their heads, like a cloud.
They wear fear like a double-faced coat:
plausible both ways.

It is a one-sided negotiation. How
do you convince a virus not to devour lungs? How
do you talk cancer into slowing down?
There is no argument to pull. No point to advance.

There is only a heaviness lodging itself in the spaces
where hopes used to live, pushing
down, down,
counting, as the number of the dead
goes up and up and up.

APRIL 5, 2020

No Trays of Food in My room. Not Today

Today,
I had dinner with my family. They gathered around the table.
I sat in the kitchen, behind the counter, MORE than six feet
apart.

They ate pasta. I swallowed my fear.
Hope crouched in the cups, waiting to be filled.

April 8, 2020

Silent Language

She doesn't hear. She reads lips.
I enter the exam room—a closed book behind a mask.
I speak:
empty spits on a blue filter. I remember
she can't hear me.

Instead, I write:
How are you doing today?
She reads. She writes back.
Back and forth. Forth and back.
She is exasperated.

She writes:
Would you skip the introductory niceties and tell me?
Were my scans better or worse?

I write: *better.*
She writes: *thank you.*

I nod. I drop my eyelids over the reddened eyes. I pause.
I open my eyes.
I see her smile behind her mask.

April 13, 2020

Warning

For S.F.

Hey Mr. Covid,
I need a word with you here.
The woman you landed in the ICU on a ventilator
is my patient.

She just finished her chemotherapy. She was cured.
I know how she struggled, how she fought.
I counted her tears.
I held her hand:
Allergic reaction. Nausea. Heaves.

I helped her pick a wig that matched the tone of her skin.

When her eyebrows fell,
we joked to disperse the gloom.
When fuzzes appeared on her bald head,
we clapped. Her eyes glittered and bloomed.

She put her jewelry back on.
Finally, she said, *I can go in public with my chin up.*

It was a party for the newly found treasures:
hair and health.

Don't dare to take that away from her.
I am warning you, Mr. Covid.
You don't know her.
You don't know anything. Blind as a bat.
Back off her lungs, back off her heart.
An army of people carried her through.
Courage, knowledge, dedication, long sleepless nights.
You can't just come from nowhere and take her just like that.
I have a word for you Mr. Covid,
Can you see how many murders and dictators
are out there in the world?
Why don't you narrow your scope and target those instead?
Leave the innocents, the poor, the strugglers, the kids,
the wives, the husbands, the lovers, the braves,
the sufferers, the fighters, the givers.
Leave them alone.

Mr. Covid,
I just learned that you had no ears to listen
and no heart.
You just took her, erased her from the map,
as if she had never been here, within my sight
only a few weeks ago.

APRIL 14, 2020

Reeling The Unreal

The boy has a nightmare.
He dreams his Mama died of the virus. He wakes.
For a moment he can't tell
which is reality and which is a dream:
the world seems unreal, yet vivid. Surreal.
Walking to his Mama's room,
he crosses the borders of quarantine.
Within six feet. She is asleep. Is she

$$\text{breathing?}$$

Mama!

She too is seeing in her sleep the vivid vision
of one of her patients who died that morning

        Of the virus
        On sweat-wet hospital bed sheets
        Under an oxygen mask
        Off the ventilator tubes
        In and around IV lines

Mama wakes. For a moment she can't tell
which is real and which is surreal.
She hears the panting of his breath,

and knows without words what's in his brain.
She pulls him closer, breaking the rules of distance.

He lays next to her.
She covers her nose and mouth with the sober-dry bed sheet.
He pulls her closer to him.
Mama kisses his head through the mask-alternate linen.
He cries. She can't.
Tears are possible transmitters.
They both know they are breaking the isolation rules,
but they don't move away
from that embrace.

April 17, 2020

An Early Drive to Work

My husband always criticizes my driving skills.
He says, on crossroads, I don't make a full stop at the sign.
Today, I do.
Stop. Full stop.
I look right. I look left.
Roads unfold, lonely and hesitant like beggar's arms.
I wait for a car to pass. None.
I wait.
I practice my patience.
None.
I have never made a full stop like that!
I turn right to a two-way lane. I dare
to drive on the two yellow lines in the middle.
I am thrilled, breaking the law.
Because now,
there are new laws to break me.
But I am safe.
No cars are coming in the opposite direction.
No cars in any direction.
No directions.
I crack the stereo up.
The car reverberates with the boom.
The Celtic lady's voice rises high and high.

May it be a knife to slice that pomegranate sky
and free those imprisoned seeds.
But the blade breaks
on the shield of the impenetrable gloom.
And the voice I need
is hidden somewhere behind the dark clouds.
None.
I lower the volume and get back in my lane,
and drive straight to
the survival of another day.

April 20, 2020

Evolution

Voices' waves rise and fold
into muffles. They yield to the omnipresent gaze:
Eyelids become lips. Blinks are the silhouettes of smiles.
Or scowls. Or pouts.
The dilation and constriction of the pupils speak—
a new language to learn.

Tiredness mutters reddened conjunctivas.
Pain speaks through the dimming twinkles of the stares.

Are we going to evolve over the years? Mask becoming a part
of the skin. Nostrils gone. Lips effaced?
The evolution of the new faces: people without mouths.
The evolution of the forced distance: people without hearts.
And the screen of the soul is a parched landscape.
A boulder in the middle
with no love lines engraved atop.

It used to be a lush spring with water and green
up there,
on that screen.

April 24, 2020

Perception

In the absence of walls, her eyes retreat and hide
behind her face. She stands at the door of her house, trying
to remember how to walk.

Cooped up within four walls, she tells me,
I lost neither my smell nor my taste,
rather it is my sense of depth perception that is gone.
I can't explain it, but I think
my eyes acquired a halt at the walls of my room;
They forgot how to see open spaces.

She sits on the stairs of the house, thinking
her vision needs to readapt
to the luminance of objects.
She blinks and blinks and blinks and waits
for her brain to converge the images in front:

Open air, trees, streets, and faraway horizon.
No walls. No walls.

It didn't take longer for her eyes to readapt;
It took much longer for her brain to re-learn,
she says,

and it still learning how
to make sense of all the new perceptions.

MAY 2, 2020
Black And White

I am old enough to remember
when we tossed away our black and white television.

Father hooked the new colored set to electricity, and
with a proud smile, pushed the button.
Images came through, bustling:
Tom and Jerry were on, I recall.
Brother and I jumped up and down and clapped.
Magic! We thought, forgetting
all characters we'd seen before
had colors since they were born.

How did we get used to black and white?
Became indifferent. Ambivalent.

We stare at black and white now,
knowing that there are colors out there. We know. We know
but they're just not coming through
yet.

MAY 23, 2020

There Is No Vaccine for Existence

The sun slurps my children's figures splashing in the pool, and
it hides behind the trees.
They go in the house. I stay outside,
reading.
I hear their showers running upstairs after a long day of fun.
Birds chirp incessantly dodging from a branch to the other.
Leaves whisper with a soft rustle.
The flowers in my garden tremble slightly in the breeze
and put their petals to snooze.
The drift brings whiffs of music from a distant backyard.
Children on the street murmur playfully.
Jumping ropes tickle the ground.
The neighbor's dog barks. A passing car blows a horn.
The dishwasher hums inside.
The water boils in the teapot on the stove. Corncobs soften.

The universe ebbs in me.

About the Author

Rana Bitar is a Syrian-American physician, poet, and writer. She earned her Master's in English and Creative Writing from Southern New Hampshire University.

Her memoir, *The Long Tale of Tears and Smiles,* was published by *Global Collective Publishers* in August 2021.

She is the author of two poetry chapbooks, *A Loaf of Bread* (*Unsolicited Press*, 2019) and the forthcoming Hold Your Breath (Unsolicited Press, 2023).

A Loaf of Bread was a finalist in the "*Concrete Wolf Chapbook Competition*" in 2017 and won an honorable mention in "*The 2017 Louis Award*" for poetry.

Hold Your Breath was selected by The National Women's History Museum to be on Exhibit for their Coronavirus Journaling Project and was featured in *The New York Times* on April 22, 2022.

Her poetry has appeared in many journals, including, *The Deadly Writers Patrol, DoveTales, Pittsburgh Poetry Review, Magnolia Review, El Portal, Pacific REVIEW, Black Coffee Review, The Phoenix, The Dewdrop, The International Human Rights Art Festival, The Charleston Anvil, Beltway Poetry Quarterly, The Sextant Review, Concrete Desert Review, The*

Nonconformist Magazine, Seeing Things: Anthology of Poetry, and The New York Times.

Her translation of Arabic poetry appeared in *The American Journal of Poetry, The Nonconformist, Illuminations, Beltway Poetry Quarterly,* and *AGNI*

Her essays have been published in *The Pharos Journal, Med Page, and Pink Panther Magazine.*

She lives in upstate NY, where she practices hematology and oncology.

Learn more at www.ranabitar.com

About Unsolicited Press

Unsolicited Press based out of Portland, Oregon and focuses on the works of the unsung and underrepresented. As a womxn-owned, all-volunteer small publisher that doesn't worry about profits as much as championing exceptional literature, we have the privilege of partnering with authors skirting the fringes of the lit world. We've worked with emerging and award-winning authors such as Shann Ray, Amy Shimshon-Santo, Brock Bhagat, Kris Amos, and John W. Bateman.

Learn more at unsolicitedpress.com. Find us on twitter and instagram.

Acknowledgments

"Self-Quarantined" appeared in *Black Coffee Review*. Spring 2020 issue

"No Trays of Food In My Room" appeared in *The Dewdrop*. May 2020

"An Early Drive to Work Appeared" in *Seeing Things: Poetry Anthology*: Bright Hills Press. June 2020

"Viral Dream" appeared in *Beltway Poetry Quarterly*, issue 21.4, volume II. Fall 2020

Index of Poems